MICHAEL P. DEMARIA

WORKBOOK for FREEDOM

Navigating The Middle Path between Order and Chaos

Copyright © 2024 by Michael P. DeMaria

All rights reserved. No part of this publication may be reproduced, stored or transmitted in any form or by any means, electronic, mechanical, photocopying, recording, scanning, or otherwise without written permission from the publisher. It is illegal to copy this book, post it to a website, or distribute it by any other means without permission.

Michael P. DeMaria asserts the moral right to be identified as the author of this work.

Michael P. DeMaria has no responsibility for the persistence or accuracy of URLs for external or third-party Internet Websites referred to in this publication and does not guarantee that any content on such Websites is, or will remain, accurate or appropriate.

Designations used by companies to distinguish their products are often claimed as trademarks. All brand names and product names used in this book and on its cover are trade names, service marks, trademarks and registered trademarks of their respective owners. The publishers and the book are not associated with any product or vendor mentioned in this book. None of the companies referenced within the book have endorsed the book.

This book does not provide professional advice or mental health services and should not be used as a substitute for consulting your medical or mental health provider. Mental and physical health conditions require diagnosis and treatment by qualified professionals. Examples and anecdotes mentioned in this book are for illustrative purposes only and do not represent actual cases or specific advice. Readers should consult their healthcare provider for personalized guidance. Do not delay seeking medical or mental health treatment because of something you have read in this book. The author of this work is not liable or responsible for any advice, treatment, diagnosis, loss, or damage resulting from the methods, information, suggestions, or teachings contained herein.

First edition

ISBN: 978-1-7379504-1-7

This book was professionally typeset on Reedsy.
Find out more at reedsy.com

Contents

About the Author   v
Introduction   vi

I   Part One: Freedom

1. The Beginning   3
2. The Causes of Suffering   6
3. A Brief History of Free Will   9
4. The Phenomenon of Polarization   12
5. Degrees of Freedom   15
6. Order and Chaos   18

II   Part Two: Acceptance

7. Acceptance and Change   23
8. Finding Non-Self   26
9. Meditation and Mindfulness   30
10. Enter the Human Shadow   34
11. Nothing Good or Bad   38
12. Methods of Acceptance   41

III Part Three: Change

13	Vision	47
14	Planning and Preparation	50
15	Self-Discipline	53
16	Problem-Solving	56
17	Persistence	60
18	Methods of Change	64

IV Part Four: Understanding

19	Generating Self-Awareness	71
20	Methods of Self-Understanding	75
21	The Middle Path Between Acceptance and Change	79

About the Author

Michael DeMaria is a Licensed Clinical Social Worker (LCSW) from Staten Island, New York. He is employed at an inpatient psychiatric hospital where he works in tandem with an interdisciplinary team to stabilize, treat, and discharge individuals with severe and persistent mental illness. Michael holds a bachelor's degree in social work and a master's degree in social work. Additionally, he is a black belt in karate and a Zen practitioner with over a decade of experience with Zen meditation.

Introduction

Welcome! You've taken a powerful step towards personal growth by choosing this workbook companion to "Freedom Navigating the Middle Path between Order and Chaos" by Michael DeMaria, LCSW. It was developed to enrich your understanding of the concepts explored in the primary text and to help you apply such knowledge to the real world. However, it can also function independently as a standalone resource to guide you through the vibrant landscape of your experiences and help you achieve more freedom in your life.

How to Make the Most of This Workbook

As you explore the chapters, you'll encounter a blend of summaries, key takeaways, self-reflection exercises, and activities that aim to deepen your understanding of the balance between order and chaos in your life. Each element is crafted to help you engage with the material in a meaningful way, providing a framework for reflection and application.

Begin with the Summaries: Before diving into the exercises, familiarize yourself with the chapter summaries. These provide context and highlight the main points you'll be working with.

Reflect on Key Takeaways: Reflect on the key takeaways after reading each summary. These are the core concepts that will be referenced throughout the exercises and activities.

Complete the Self-Reflection Exercises: These exercises are designed to help you apply the concepts to your personal experiences. Take your time, write out your thoughts, and be as honest as possible. The more sincere your answers, the more you'll benefit from the process.

Participate in the Activities: The activities are practical applications of the workbook's concepts. Whether it's a meditation practice, journaling, or a lifestyle modification, these activities are meant to solidify your understanding and bring the ideas into your daily life.

Revisit When Needed: This workbook is not meant to be completed once and set aside (although that's possible too if you wish). Return to it periodically, especially as you encounter new challenges or wish to reflect on your growth. Repeating exercises and activities with fresh insights can be incredibly rewarding.

Take it at Your Own Pace: There's no need to rush. Progress through the workbook at a pace that feels comfortable and beneficial for you.

Use as a Standalone or Supplement: Once again, while this workbook complements the teachings found in the main text, it is also structured to be beneficial on its own. Whether you've read the corresponding chapters or not, you can still find value in the exercises and reflections contained within.

I

Part One: Freedom

1

The Beginning

In this chapter, I invite you on a journey through my personal history, beginning in the harsh landscape of a childhood marked by emotional, physical, and psychological abuse. This early adversity laid the groundwork for a rebellious and tumultuous adolescence, characterized by bullying, a life-altering accident, and intense struggles with mental health and substance abuse.

As we delve deeper, I share a pivotal moment that transformed my trajectory—a discovery that ignited a curiosity about the mind's transformative power and led me to meditation. This practice opened the door to many other transformative methods, bringing profound personal changes and propelling me toward pursuing education and eventually a career dedicated to mental health.

Throughout the chapter, we explore not only the challenges but also the crucial methods that fueled my recovery and growth. This journey underscores an important message: despite disempowering views that often confine individuals to their past, we all possess the innate capacity to transcend our circumstances and shape our destinies.

Ultimately, the insights gleaned from my experiences offer hope and guidance to others facing similar struggles. Recognizing that transformation is within reach, and that each of us has the power to redefine our paths, provides not only comfort but a call to action. My story is not just a personal narrative but a testament to the power of resilience and a call to all who struggle to embrace their agency and shape their own destiny.

Key Takeaways:

1. Early adversity and trauma can have profound, long-lasting effects but do not determine the path we ultimately take.
2. Personal responsibility and the will to change are critical components in overcoming negative cycles and addiction.
3. Free will is not just a philosophical concept but a tangible force that shapes our personal destinies and well-being.
4. Empowerment and the exertion of will are possible even when it feels like our paths are set, allowing for personal transformation.
5. The belief in our ability to change is a prerequisite for actual change to occur.

Self-Reflection Exercises:

1. Think of a time when you felt you had no choice. How did this impact your mental health, and how did you find your way back to a sense of freedom?

2. Consider the concept of "psychological freedom" even when you're in a tough situation, like a job you don't enjoy, or a difficult relationship. Can you think of a situation where you felt free despite external limitations?

Activities:

1. Meditation Practice: Start a daily meditation routine, beginning with just five minutes a day, and gradually increase the time as you become more comfortable.
2. Gratitude Letter: Write a letter of gratitude to someone who has positively influenced your journey, even if you won't send it. This can shift your focus from past hardships to the support and kindness you've received, which fosters a sense of liberation from negative experiences.

2

The Causes of Suffering

Feeling powerless is not merely a state of discomfort, it is a pervasive and oppressive weight on the soul that, left unaddressed, can have a significant negative impact on our well-being. Drawing from both my personal experiences and professional practice, I explore the detrimental consequences that can stem from a perceived lack of control over one's life. These feelings of powerlessness are not just unsettling; they are often the precursor to a host of negative psychological outcomes, including addiction, unhealthy eating habits, depression, and even suicidal thoughts.

We, as individuals, face a daily reality where our sense of autonomy can be challenged or undermined. Throughout the chapter, I discuss the importance of self-determination and autonomy, supported by extensive research linking these elements to enhanced well-being, life satisfaction, and healthier lifestyles, while also reducing the risk of trauma-related conditions.

Further, I examine the role of free will in our moral and ethical landscapes. The belief in our ability to choose freely is not only central to personal growth but is also imperative for the moral health of society at large. Case studies presented in the chapter illustrate how fostering a sense of personal agency can lead to more responsible and ethical decision-making, positively impacting our communities and social interactions.

By understanding and nurturing our intrinsic power to make choices, we can counter feelings of powerlessness and their many ramifications. This chapter not only illuminates these crucial connections but also offers actionable advice and insights that can empower us to lead more fulfilled and autonomous lives. In embracing our personal agency, we open the door to not only surviving but thriving in the face of life's challenges.

Key Takeaways:

1. The sense of being trapped or powerless can significantly contribute to mental and emotional suffering.
2. Self-determination and autonomy are crucial for psychological well-being and can mitigate the impact of stressful events.
3. Belief in free will is associated with moral behavior and social responsibility; conversely, disbelief in free will can lead to unethical actions.
4. It is important to encourage individuals to feel in control of their lives for their personal mental health and for the well-being of society.

Self-Reflection Exercise:

1. Consider the areas of your life where you feel a strong sense of autonomy. How does this influence your well-being?

Activities:

1. Journaling Exercise: Write about an aspect of your life where you desire more control. Detail steps you could take to increase your sense of autonomy in this area.
2. Self-Determination Plan: Create a personal action plan that outlines specific goals for increasing autonomy in different aspects of your life, including career, relationships, and personal growth.

3

A Brief History of Free Will

On our exploration of free will, we traverse the landscape of human thought, from ancient Greek philosophy to modern physics and neuroscience. We begin with early thinkers' grappling with autonomy and destiny, setting the stage for a deeper inquiry into freedom and the power of choice.

We delve into the transformative impacts of Newton's laws and Einstein's theory of relativity, introducing a deterministic universe governed by immutable laws. This raises profound questions about our choices—are they truly ours, or merely outcomes of cosmic rules? The tension between determinism and the belief in free will is further complicated by neuroscience studies like the Libet Experiments, which challenge our understanding of when and how decisions are (seemingly) made.

We explore the age-old debate between free will and determinism, examining how our perception of ourselves as either architects of our destiny or actors following a script profoundly influences our actions and decisions.

Ultimately, we encounter the notion of compatibilism, a compelling perspective suggesting that free will and determinism are not mutually exclusive. Compatibilism offers a middle path, proposing that our understanding of free will does not require an all-or-nothing approach. Instead, there are moments when we are free to make choices and others when our freedom is constrained.

By embracing this nuanced view, we can find greater balance and freedom in our lives. This chapter not only deepens our understanding of a complex philosophical issue but also empowers us to reconsider how we make choices and perceive our control over our destinies. Through this lens, we see how taking the middle path in understanding free will, and indeed in many other areas of life, can lead us to a richer, more liberated existence.

Key Takeaways:

1. The concept of free will has been debated for centuries, with various schools of thought offering differing opinions and insights.
2. Scientific developments have both challenged and informed our views on free will, suggesting that some of our decision-making may occur unconsciously.
3. The Libet Experiments suggest that while our conscious mind might not initiate actions, it may still have the power to inhibit them.
4. Compatibilism, a form of taking a middle path, offers a way to view free will as compatible with a universe governed by fixed laws, without ignoring scientific truths.

Self-Reflection Exercises:

1. Consider a recent decision you made. Reflect on the factors that influenced this decision and whether you believe it was made freely or was determined by previous influences.
2. Ponder situations where you've felt a strong sense of agency. How do these compare to instances where you've felt your actions were determined by factors outside your control?
3. Reflect on a time when you changed your mind at the last moment about a significant choice. What prompted the change, and do you think this was an exercise of free will or a response to subconscious influences?

Activity:

1. Mindful Decision Awareness: Engage in a week-long mindfulness exercise where you note significant decisions you make, categorizing them as either "impulsive" or "deliberate." Note the reasoning or lack of it behind each choice. Review your notes after the week to see how many decisions were made with deliberate thought versus those made automatically. This aims to raise awareness of our unconscious decision drivers and assess our conscious control. It also investigates mindfulness's role in enhancing free will by increasing conscious decision-making.

4

The Phenomenon of Polarization

Polarization, the tendency to divide the world into black and white, is a deeply ingrained human trait. This simplification can be advantageous in situations demanding swift action, as our evolutionary history demonstrates. However, a closer examination reveals how this inclination can distort our understanding of reality, particularly in social and political realms.

Polarization fuels conflict, obscures nuanced solutions, and fosters societal divisions. Throughout history, deeply rooted divisions have led to prolonged disputes and hindered resolutions. By delving into the psychological underpinnings of polarization—including defense mechanisms like projection and the influence of group dynamics—we gain insight into why individuals and societies gravitate toward extremes.

Ultimately, this chapter challenges us to confront our own biases and seek out the rich terrain that lies beyond polar extremes. By understanding the roots and repercussions of polarization, we can work towards solutions that embrace the full spectrum of human perspectives. In a world increasingly divided, this understanding is not just enlightening; it's essential.

Key Takeaways:

1. Polarization, or the classification of the world into dual opposites, aids decision-making but often fails to capture the complex nature of reality.
2. Philosophical and historical perspectives highlight the fallibility of all-or-nothing thinking and the existence of spectrums rather than distinct categories.
3. Polarization can have detrimental effects on society by exacerbating conflicts and preventing compromise.
4. Psychological theories suggest that polarization is a defense mechanism influenced by the need for social cohesion and fear of rejection within group dynamics.
5. Acknowledging the continuum on which concepts like free will exist can offer a more nuanced understanding and possibly enhance our capacity for freedom.

Self-Reflection Exercises:

1. Reflect on a recent decision you made using all-or-nothing thinking. Write down the two options you considered and brainstorm at least three "middle-ground" alternatives.
2. Consider a polarized belief you hold. Write about the origins of this belief and challenge yourself to find valid arguments on the opposing side.
3. Think about a time when being part of a group influenced you to take a more extreme position. Reflect on the desire for acceptance and consider how you might approach a

similar situation differently in the future.

Activities:

1. Create a spectrum chart for a polarized topic (e.g., political stance, moral judgments). Mark where you currently stand, and then mark where you might stand if you considered a more nuanced perspective.
2. Engage in a dialectical discussion with someone who holds an opposing view on a subject. Practice active listening and aim to find common ground.
3. Explore a historical conflict caused by polarization. What potential middle paths were available but not taken in this conflict? How might these alternative approaches potentially have led to a more peaceful resolution?

5

Degrees of Freedom

In this chapter, we explore the multifaceted concept of free will, presenting it as a spectrum encompassing varying degrees of freedom, each reflecting a deeper level of autonomy and self-determination. As we progress, we uncover how the development of free will is not only possible but essential for fostering a purposeful and fulfilling life.

We begin with the first degree of free will—basic freedom from external restrictions. This foundational level represents the absence of constraints that prevent us from acting according to our basic desires and needs. It's the freedom to act without physical or overt psychological barriers, an essential starting point for any discussion on free will.

Advancing to the second degree, we encounter the capacity to make choices based on higher desires, not merely on instinctual urges. This stage introduces a more refined form of freedom, where one is free not only from external constraints but also begins to exercise control over internal compulsions and reactions. At this level, we have the freedom to pursue goals that reflect our values and aspirations rather than mere survival instincts.

The peak of this spectrum is the third degree of free will, which I equate with autonomy. Autonomy represents the ultimate form of free will, where individuals possess the freedom to self-determine their life's course. This highest level involves making informed and reflective choices that align with one's deeper values and long-term objectives. It is about being the author of one's life narrative, not merely responding to the environment or internal impulses.

This chapter argues that while free will is an inherent aspect of the human experience, its fuller expression must be cultivated through deliberate effort and reflection. Cultivating free will is crucial for transitioning from a state of passive existence or despondency to a state of intentional living. By developing our capacity for higher degrees of free will, we enhance our well-being, enabling more active engagement with life's opportunities and challenges.

Key Takeaways:

1. Freedom is a nuanced spectrum, encompassing basic freedom from constraints to autonomy and self-determination.
2. The spectrum progresses from simple freedom from restrictions to the ability to inhibit unhelpful urges and act on

higher desires. For instance, we might inhibit the impulse to indulge in unhealthy snacks and instead make conscious dietary choices based on long-term health goals.
3. Autonomy grants us the power to self-determine their lives, fostering intentional living and purposeful choices. This might involve consciously choosing a career aligned with our passions and actively shaping our professional trajectory.
4. Developing more freedom will significantly enhance well-being, transcending aimlessness and leading to a more fulfilling existence.

Self-Reflection Exercise:

1. Think about a recent decision where you used willpower. What higher-order desire did you honor, and how did it align with your values?

Activity:

1. Develop a personal mission statement that reflects your highest desires and intentions. Use this to guide your decisions for a week, noting any shifts in your sense of freedom or purpose. If you find it helpful, frame it somewhere you can see it on a regular basis.

6

Order and Chaos

This chapter plunges us into the heart of a timeless paradox: the intricate dance between order and chaos. How can we reconcile the human need for structure and predictability with life's inherent unpredictability and change? Through a blend of personal anecdotes and historical references, I demonstrate how navigating this middle path allows us to harness the strengths of both order and chaos.

We explore the symbolism of order and chaos across various cultural and religious traditions. We examine their myriad representations: from the structured harmony of Confucian philosophy to the temperamental whims of Greek gods, from the biblical tale of creation from void to the Hindu concept of cosmic cycles of creation and destruction. These narratives collectively underscore a universal understanding of the world as an interplay between structured predictability and transformative unpredictability.

We then transition to modern psychological theories, which

emphasize the necessity of balancing stability and adaptability in our lives. By integrating ancient wisdom with contemporary thought, the path toward achieving this delicate balance is illuminated. Harnessing the strengths of order and chaos can help in cultivating inner freedom, resilience, and the ability to adapt to life's ever-changing circumstances. Ultimately, order and chaos are not opposing forces but catalysts for self-discovery and personal transformation.

Key Takeaways:

1. The concepts of order and chaos serve as fundamental structures of reality, influencing our understanding and actions.
2. Polarization, or the division into extremes, limits our ability to see the benefits of balance and middle paths.
3. Historical and philosophical teachings, from Buddhism's middle way to Aristotle's golden mean, emphasize the importance of moderation.
4. Achieving balance, or following the middle path, is integral to personal well-being and can lead to a more autonomous and fulfilling life.

Self-Reflection Exercises:

1. Reflect on a recent situation where you found yourself leaning too far toward 'order' or 'chaos.' How did this affect your sense of balance and well-being?
2. Think about a time when you were forced to shift your 'position' in life. What caused the shift, and what did you learn from it?

Activities:

1. Draw a yin-yang symbol to represent areas of order and chaos in your life. Label the sections with specific aspects of your life that embody order (e.g., routines, organization) and chaos (e.g., spontaneity, uncertainty). Reflect on these areas and identify where you might seek greater balance to enhance your overall well-being.
2. Commit to a week of consciously seeking balance in your daily choices. For instance, balance your work commitments with relaxation and leisure activities. At the end of each day, journal any changes you notice in your mental state, mood, or overall life satisfaction. Reflect on the impact of this balanced approach at the end of the week.

II

Part Two: Acceptance

7

Acceptance and Change

In Chapter Seven: Acceptance and Change, we explore the dynamic interplay between acceptance and change, often viewed as opposing forces in personal development. Throughout my life and professional practice, I've observed a growing divide between these concepts, which hinders true autonomy and harmony. This chapter aims to bridge that gap by advocating for a balanced integration of acceptance and change.

Our modern era's vast access to information has led to varied interpretations of self-improvement, pushing many to choose between radical acceptance or relentless change. Drawing from my experiences as a Zen practitioner, martial artist, and clinical social worker, I argue that true balance and personal growth come from integrating both acceptance and change, much like balancing order and chaos.

Today, messages promoting self-acceptance and self-compassion often lack practical guidance. True acceptance is not passive resignation but a profound understanding and acknowledgment of reality. It's a tool to be used alongside the drive for change, depending on the situation. Self-acceptance, frequently misunderstood as self-pity or indifference, is actually an act of self-love and a foundation for personal growth.

Therapeutic settings highlight the power of acceptance-based strategies. For example, Acceptance and Commitment Therapy (ACT) teaches mindfulness and reduces emotional reactivity, promoting psychological flexibility. Genuine acceptance facilitates change by allowing us to grow authentically, free from the pressures of unrealistic standards. Figures like Carl Rogers advocate for embracing our inherent worth and engaging in life authentically.

Dialectical Behavior Therapy (DBT) underscores the importance of balancing rationality and emotionality. DBT's concept of the "wise mind" exemplifies the integration of acceptance and change, fostering equilibrium crucial for managing intense emotions and making thoughtful decisions. Additionally, the concept of "ironic rebound" shows that attempts to suppress thoughts make them more persistent, highlighting the need for acceptance to reduce mental struggles and achieve inner peace.

In conclusion, Chapter Seven presents acceptance and change as complementary tools essential for personal growth and well-being. By understanding and integrating these concepts, we can navigate life's challenges more effectively, fostering a balanced and fulfilling existence. The upcoming chapters will delve into methods from various psychological and spiritual traditions, offering practical steps to cultivate acceptance and achieve inner harmony.

Key Takeaways:

1. Acceptance and change are not opposing teams but complementary tools for personal development.
2. Genuine acceptance is an active process involving understanding ourselves and our circumstances without self-neglect or indifference.
3. Acceptance strategies are used in therapeutic settings to foster mental health and resilience.
4. The journey toward true self-acceptance is a prerequisite for achieving inner peace and autonomy.

Self-Reflection Exercises:

1. Reflect on instances where you may have mistaken giving up for acceptance in your own life.
2. Consider situations where you might benefit from acceptance versus change, and why.
3. Think about the balance of acceptance and change in your life—are you leaning too far to one side?

Activities:

1. Write about a time when acceptance led to positive change in your life.
2. Practice a mindfulness exercise focusing on accepting your current thoughts and emotions without judgment.

8

Finding Non-Self

The concept of non-self, or "anātman" is a cornerstone of Eastern philosophy. Have you ever paused to consider the nature of your "self"? We often take our personal identity for granted, spending our lives constructing and defending this sense of who we are. But what if this is merely an illusion?

Our culture bombards us with messages about "finding yourself" and "soul searching," implying there's a hidden, true self beneath the surface. However, the doctrine of anātman challenges this notion, suggesting that there is no static, unchanging self. Rather, our identity is a dynamic collection of transient, interrelated experiences, constantly influenced by our social environment and personal interactions.

Embracing the concept of non-self can be a liberating experience. It allows us to release the attachments and clinging that cause so much suffering. In Buddhism, attachment to the self is seen as the root of psychological anguish. By recognizing the impermanence of self, we can alleviate existential fears and live more harmoniously with the transitory nature of existence.

Meditative practices, such as mindfulness meditation and Zen koans, offer a direct path to experiencing the non-self. The Zen Buddhist experience of "satori," or sudden enlightenment, is a powerful example. During satori, the sense of "I" dissolves, and one feels an inseparable connection to the universe. This direct experience, much like the Zen saying, "A finger pointing to the moon is not the moon," emphasizes the importance of experiencing reality firsthand rather than relying solely on intellectual understanding.

Let us then reframe the idea of self-discovery. Instead of seeking a permanent self, we should embrace the ongoing process of becoming. We are dynamic beings, constantly evolving through our experiences and choices. The doctrine of non-self invites us to create ourselves anew, shedding the limitations of a fixed identity. This perspective empowers us to navigate the ever-changing flow of life, continually shaping and reshaping our identity in harmony with our environment and experiences, ultimately leading to greater peace and fulfillment.

Key Takeaways:

1. The sense of a permanent, individual self is a deep-seated human belief, but Eastern philosophies challenge this notion with the concept of non-self (anātman).
2. Social environment and interactions heavily influence our

sense of self, often altering our behaviors and desires in ways we may not consciously recognize.
3. Physical and neurological investigations reveal that personal identity cannot be pinpointed to any specific part of the body or brain, suggesting that the self is not a constant entity.
4. Clinging to the concept of a stable self can lead to suffering; understanding non-self is a path to acceptance and liberation from existential fears.
5. The concept of non-self allows for a liberating perspective on life, emphasizing the dynamic process of self-creation rather than the discovery of a pre-existing identity.

Self-Reflection Exercises:

1. Reflect on the last time you adapted your behavior to fit a social situation. Did it feel like a change in your identity or merely a response to the environment?
2. Contemplate instances where your desires or interests have been shaped by those around you. How does this affect your understanding of your 'self'?
3. Consider the idea that your consciousness and sense of self disappear during deep, dreamless sleep. What does this imply about the continuity of your personal identity?

Activities:

1. Create a 'map' of your social influences by listing the five people you spend the most time with and noting how each has impacted your beliefs and behaviors.
2. Find a quiet space, set aside a few minutes, and settle into

a comfortable seated position. Now, focus on your body and surroundings, and notice the sensations at the surface of your skin. Imagine the boundary dissolving, merging your awareness with the environment. Write down your observations—could you find a clear boundary between yourself and the world? If not, what happens when you look deeper? Continue to delve deeper until you see how you are inseparable from the world around you.

9

Meditation and Mindfulness

In this chapter, we examine the ancient practice of meditation and its contemporary application known as mindfulness. Originating from early Indian religions, especially Buddhism, meditation has been embraced by Western psychology as a therapeutic technique. Mindfulness, integral to a multitude of psychotherapies, is used to improve mental health. We explore how mindfulness not only strengthens acceptance and independence but also connects deeply with our ability to manage our emotions effectively.

The chapter primarily discusses Zen meditation, or Zazen, which emphasizes focused awareness on the present moment without judgment. Zazen involves sitting still and counting breaths, teaching acceptance of the present moment and the transient nature of thoughts and emotions. This practice reveals the mind's tendency to dwell on past failures or future anxieties, and it helps us detach from these ruminations, fostering patience and tolerance. I share insights into the science behind meditation, focusing on its profound impact on the brain—especially the prefrontal cortex—which plays a crucial role in enhancing our decision-making abilities and self-control. Through a blend of scientific research and stories from personal experiences, I highlight the transformative power of meditation in achieving mental clarity, mastering self-regulation, and boosting overall wellness.

A vivid analogy, the "forest pool," illustrates how meditation can help us see the world, and "ourselves" more clearly. This analogy compares our minds to a forest pool. Our thoughts and emotions are like the sediment that muddies the water when disturbed by outside forces (just as wind and rain might disturb a pool). When agitated, we lose clarity, and our decisions often make things worse. Zazen meditation, with its focus on the breath, is like patiently waiting for the water to clear. By remaining still and concentrating on the present moment, we allow the "sediment" of the mind to settle, revealing a clearer view of the world and ourselves. These insights into meditation are not just about theory; but rather they are an invitation to experience its benefits firsthand, making it a part of your own journey.

The chapter further explores how meditation enhances emotion regulation and increases autonomy by strengthening the prefrontal cortex, reducing amygdala activity, and improving self-control. Studies show that meditation can increase gray matter in brain regions associated with executive function. Personal anecdotes illustrate the transformative power of meditation in managing emotions and impulsivity. The chapter concludes that beyond its numerous physical, mental, and emotional benefits, meditation offers liberation from the confines of the mind, providing a profound sense of peace and self-acceptance.

Key Takeaways:

1. Meditation, particularly Zazen, is a practice focused on mindfulness or bringing one's attention to the present moment without judgment.
2. Emotional regulation is closely tied to brain regions like the prefrontal cortex, and meditation has been shown to improve this through neuroplasticity.
3. Regular meditation practice can result in increased gray matter in the brain, better emotion regulation, and reduced stress response.
4. Mindfulness can transform one's reactivity to situations, offering increased mental clarity and the freedom to choose how to respond to life's challenges.

Self-Reflection Exercises:

1. Consider a recurrent negative thought. Apply nonjudgmental observation to it, noting its presence and letting it go without further engagement.
2. Focus on the here and now and notice the sensation of being fully present. Can you see how concerns about the past or future dissipate in the current moment?

Activities

1. Practice Zazen meditation for 10 minutes daily, focusing on your breath and returning to it each time your mind wanders.
2. Journaling exercise: Write about a recent situation where you reacted impulsively. How might mindfulness have changed your response?

10

Enter the Human Shadow

Chapter Ten, "Enter the Human Shadow," involves the concept of the "shadow" self, introduced by psychologist Carl Jung. Initially a follower of Sigmund Freud, Jung eventually developed his own theories, including the idea of the human "shadow." This shadow represents the hidden aspects of our personality that we often ignore or reject—desires, impulses, and emotions that don't align with our self-image.

This internal conflict can result in a polarized personality, where we act differently in various settings, causing stress and discomfort. Jung's theory of the shadow provides a framework for integrating these aspects to achieve a more balanced and authentic self. He believed that everyone has a shadow containing both positive and negative qualities. Suppressing these aspects leads to psychological suffering and inner turmoil. Instead of trying to eliminate the shadow, Jung advocated for expressing it healthily, preventing it from growing uncontrollably and causing harm. This process, called individuation, involves accepting and integrating the shadow into our conscious selves, allowing us to function more freely and genuinely.

Personal anecdotes illustrate the practical application of these ideas. I share experiences of burnout from over-discipline and the realization that rest and indulgence are crucial for balance. By naming and understanding the conflicting parts of myself, such as the disciplined "monk" and the chaotic "wolf," I describe my journey toward self-acceptance and integration. This process reduces internal conflict and leads to a more authentic and fulfilling life. The chapter emphasizes that embracing our shadow allows us to be truly ourselves, blending our ordered and chaotic sides into a harmonious whole. This integration helps us navigate social conventions without losing our individuality, fostering genuine self-acceptance and freedom.

The chapter also includes personal anecdotes from psychotherapy to illustrate the tension we all face: the tug-of-war between conforming to societal norms and honoring our true selves. This journey is not about rejecting social norms entirely but finding a way to live within them while still honoring the complex, sometimes contradictory aspects of our nature. By embracing our shadow, we learn to see ourselves as whole, accepting the good, the bad, and everything in between. This chapter serves as a guide to understanding that authenticity involves acknowledging all parts of ourselves, including those we might prefer to keep in the dark. Through this acceptance, we can live more fully, embracing a life of authenticity and depth.

Key Takeaways:

1. The human shadow contains both positive and negative aspects, often suppressed due to societal expectations.
2. Self-acceptance and integration of the shadow are important aspects of mental health.
3. It is essential to find a balance between conforming to social conventions and expressing one's individuality.
4. Suppression of the shadow can lead to psychological turmoil.
5. True self-individuation is achieved when one embraces and controls the disowned aspects of themselves.

Self-Reflection Exercises:

1. Reflect on aspects of your personality you feel you have to suppress in various social settings. Are there more acceptable ways to express these traits?
2. Consider a recent situation where you felt a strong emotion, like anger. How did you handle it, and how could you have managed it in a way that's true to your feelings but still socially appropriate?

Activities:

1. Reflect on aspects of your emotional life that you feel you have to bottle up. What are some safe ways to express these feelings? This week commit to trying one of these methods until you feel you have provided a healthy outlet for aspects of yourself longing to be expressed. Some

examples include creative activities like writing a song, poem, or painting. You might also try physical exercises like dancing, kickboxing or walking while focusing on your feelings.
2. Keep a dream journal to record your dreams upon waking. Analyze these for recurring themes that might represent hidden or suppressed parts of your personality.

Note: These activities may bring up some difficult emotions. If you find they bring up more than you can handle alone, it's good to seek guidance from a qualified therapist.

11

Nothing Good or Bad

This chapter invites us to consider a powerful truth: sometimes our greatest growth comes from accepting our deepest pain. By exploring what it means to accept suffering, I demonstrate how acceptance, even in life's most challenging circumstances, can open doors to transformation. Our perception—how we see the world—can turn a painful experience into a catalyst for growth, rather than an anchor dragging us down.

We delve into the factors contributing to trauma, acknowledging that elements such as lack of social support, genetics, perceived life threat, and prior trauma history play significant roles. These factors can make some people more vulnerable to PTSD and other mental illnesses. However, the chapter highlights the power of personal agency in shaping one's perception of traumatic events. Those who find purpose during adversity and maintain a sense of personal control are less likely to develop long-term trauma symptoms.

I explore the elements that contribute to traumatic stress

and the factors that build long-term resilience, which is key to recovering from setbacks, chronic stressors, and major adversities. Retaining our power to choose, even in difficult situations, is vital to our well-being. Drawing on ideas from Stoic philosophy and Buddhist teachings, I show how changing our thoughts and finding purpose within hardship can lead to remarkable personal transformation.

The chapter also discusses the concept of post-traumatic growth, where individuals find transformative meaning in their suffering by consciously seeking benefits and learning from their experiences. Studies show that this shift in perspective can lead to better relationships, increased resilience, and improved mental health outcomes.

Finally, the chapter explores "The Myth of Sisyphus" as a metaphor for finding freedom and happiness through acceptance, even in seemingly unacceptable circumstances. Ultimately, acceptance is not about passive resignation but about actively choosing how to perceive and respond to life's challenges. By embracing adversity as a source of growth and learning, we can transform suffering into a powerful catalyst for personal development and resilience. Through acceptance, we gain the ability to find purpose even in the most extreme circumstances, thereby improving our overall well-being and understanding of life.

Key Takeaways:

1. Acceptance of pain is a complex process, especially concerning extreme and uncontrollable life events.

2. Perception and personal agency can significantly influence whether an event results in trauma or transformation.
3. Factors like social support, genetics, and childhood trauma affect one's susceptibility to PTSD and other mental health issues.
4. Stoic and Buddhist philosophies offer insight into using cognitive reframing and purpose-seeking as tools for personal growth.
5. Post-traumatic growth is possible and involves finding benefit and meaning in adversity, as illustrated through the metaphor of Sisyphus.

Self-Reflection Exercises:

1. Reflect on a difficult event in your life and identify any growth or learning that came from it.
2. Consider your perceptions of control and agency during challenging times; how have these perceptions influenced your outcomes?

Activities:

1. Create a personal timeline of a traumatic event, highlighting moments where you exhibited agency or control.
2. Develop a "benefit-finding" journal, documenting daily instances where you find positive aspects within negative experiences.

12

Methods of Acceptance

In this chapter, we explore practical techniques to embody acceptance, a principle that liberates us from resistance and struggle. Drawing from both ancient traditions and contemporary practices, we offer unique pathways to cultivate acceptance.

We begin with Dzogchen, a Tibetan Buddhist practice promoted by Sam Harris. Dzogchen emphasizes experiencing non-duality directly by turning attention inward to observe the mind itself. This practice reveals our thoughts and emotions as fleeting, helping us detach from negative emotions and see them as transient rather than permanent.

Next, we explore See Hear Feel, a technique by Shinzen Young. This method involves labeling sensory experiences—sights, sounds, and feelings—as they arise, offering a straightforward way to stay present and fostering deeper awareness and acceptance of our current state.

Yoga integrates physical exertion with meditative practice, enhancing our ability to manage stress and cultivate calm. It teaches us to synchronize breath with movement, turning physical exercise into a form of moving meditation that supports mental and emotional balance.

Gratitude practice encourages us to focus on what we have rather than what we lack. By writing down things we're grateful for each night, we train our minds to seek out positivity, improving overall well-being and mental health.

Zazen, or seated meditation, involves focusing on the breath and maintaining correct posture. This disciplined approach helps cultivate stillness and acceptance, observing the wandering mind without judgment.

Relaxation strategies, such as progressive muscle relaxation and diaphragmatic breathing, offer immediate stress reduction. These techniques help identify and release physical tension, promoting a state of calm that is physiologically incompatible with worry.

Floatation therapy, where one floats in a sensory deprivation tank, provides profound relaxation by reducing sensory input, leading to mental clarity and reduced anxiety.

Breathing techniques like 2:1 breathing and square breathing demonstrate the power of controlled breath in managing stress. By extending our exhalations or practicing even breaths, we activate the parasympathetic nervous system, lowering heart rate and blood pressure.

Massage therapy is highlighted as a natural way to relieve tension and foster psychological well-being. The therapeutic touch mimics the nurturing and security we experienced as infants, reminding us of the primal need for human connection and physical comfort.

Each method offers a distinct pathway to acceptance, showing that this state of mind can be cultivated through various practices. Whether through meditation, mindful breathing, physical exercise, or gratitude, these techniques help us embrace the present moment and navigate life's challenges with greater ease and resilience. Integrating these practices into our daily lives enhances our understanding and experience of acceptance, leading to a more peaceful and fulfilling existence.

Key Takeaways:

1. Acceptance is key to experiencing freedom in one's life and can be cultivated through various practices.
2. Dzogchen, a Tibetan Buddhist tradition, focuses on experiencing non-duality and observing the mind itself.
3. The See Hear Feel technique helps label sensory experiences in the present moment, aiding mindfulness and improving emotional intelligence.
4. Yoga combines physical exertion with mindfulness, promoting stress management and mental well-being.
5. Simple relaxation strategies and breathing techniques like diaphragmatic breathing, floatation therapy, 2:1 breathing,

square breathing, and massage therapy can induce the relaxation response, combating stress and anxiety.

Self-Reflection Exercises:

1. Consider a situation where you felt a strong emotion. How might seeing this emotion as temporary change your response to similar situations in the future.
2. Identify a relaxation technique you haven't tried before. How could incorporating this into your routine potentially benefit your mental health?

Activities:

1. Practice Dzogchen by attempting to observe the mind for five minutes, using the "headless way" or turning attention inwards.
2. Engage in a See Hear Feel meditation session. Spend ten minutes noting sensory experiences and gently labeling them.
3. Write down three things you're grateful for tonight and reflect on how focusing on these positive aspects affects your mood.
4. Try a basic yoga session, focusing on synchronizing your breath with your movements, and observe how this affects your mental state.
5. Perform a relaxation exercise, like diaphragmatic breathing or square breathing, before bed and note any changes in your sleep quality.

III

Part Three: Change

13

Vision

In our fast-paced society, we're constantly bombarded with messages promoting productivity, hard work, and the accumulation of wealth and material possessions as the keys to happiness. Advertisements perpetuate the notion that true happiness stems from physical beauty and material success. This creates a distorted view of change and leaves us grappling with how to genuinely free ourselves from suffering.

In this chapter, we explore the difference between "self-help," which targets specific problems, and "personal growth," which is about continuous improvement. Indeed, there is significant overlap between psychology and self-improvement. Self-help typically addresses managing functional impairments, often without professional assistance, while personal growth aims at improving an already functional life. Despite these distinctions, many methods from self-help and psychotherapy are beneficial for personal growth.

For individuals to change successfully and grow, they need several fundamental traits: vision, the ability to pre-plan, self-discipline, self-knowledge, problem-solving skills, and persistence. Knowing where you want to go (vision), planning your course, resisting temptations (self-discipline), understanding your potential (self-knowledge), developing necessary skills (problem-solving), and maintaining steadfastness (persistence) are essential attributes for personal achievement.

Vision, in particular, stands as the cornerstone of change, improvement, or goal accomplishment. Without a clear understanding of who you want to be, you remain aimless, trapped in ambiguity and missed opportunities. Envisioning your desired self provides direction and purpose, much like a map and compass guide a sailor. This clarity allows your life to take form and shape, giving you a fighting chance to achieve your goals.

Buddha's insight that "our life is shaped by our mind; we become what we think" underscores the power of vision. Just as the skyscrapers of the New York City skyline began as mere thoughts, the person you wish to become starts as a vision in your mind. By carefully planning our futures with the same enthusiasm as we do for our vacations or weekend plans, we can leverage our unique human capability for detailed forethought and future planning. This approach allows us to craft a meaningful and fulfilling life, embracing the transformative power of vision and purposeful thinking. This chapter sets the stage for a deeper dive into self-knowledge in the following chapters.

Key Takeaways:

1. A clear vision is like a roadmap for personal change. Without it, it's easy to get lost or sidetracked on the way to achieving our goals.
2. True fulfillment isn't found in chasing possessions or outward appearances.
3. While "self-help" focuses on overcoming specific challenges, "personal growth" is about reaching our full potential.
4. Successful change relies on several key ingredients: vision, planning, self-discipline, self-knowledge, problem-solving, and the determination to keep going.
5. Developing a clear vision for the person we want to become gives our lives direction and turns our dreams into reality.

Self-Reflection Exercises:

1. Write down how the societal portrayal of success has influenced your definition of happiness and personal growth.
2. Identify and record instances in your life where you've successfully applied the six traits for change. What was the outcome?

Activity:

1. Draft a personal "map" that outlines your goals and the steps needed to achieve them.

14

Planning and Preparation

Chapter Fourteen, "Planning and Preparation," explores how fear can both protect and limit us. We all have innate fears – think of the jolt you feel stepping off an unexpectedly high curb. These are critical for survival. But we also develop conditioned fears, anxieties learned over time that might become exaggerated or hold us back.

Next, the chapter explores the power of visualization as well as the notion of extinction. Visualization involves mentally rehearsing scenarios to prepare our brains for real-life situations. Supported by neuroscience, visualization can significantly boost our readiness for various challenges. Extinction, on the other hand, involves reducing fear through controlled exposure, a method used in exposure therapy. By facing our fears in a safe setting, we can lessen their influence on our lives.

Further, we examine fear prophylaxis, underscoring the importance of preparation and exposure in overcoming fear. A notable example used is astronaut Chris Hadfield's intensive training for spaceflight, which effectively prepared him to handle fears in the unpredictable environment of space.

Lastly, I consider mortality salience—the contemplation of death. While it might seem somber, this reflection can actually encourage a more engaged and fearless approach to life, inspiring us to live with more purpose and less apprehension.

These insights aim to equip us with the tools and understanding needed to confront our fears and seize the opportunities for growth that await beyond them.

Key Takeaways:

1. Fear comes in two main types: innate fears, which are natural and necessary, and conditioned fears, which can be unnecessary and even debilitating.
2. Since the brain often can't tell the difference between what's real and what's imagined, practicing scenarios in your mind can effectively prepare you for real-life challenges and help manage fear.
3. Repeated exposure to what frightens us (in a safe setting), is crucial in reducing fear responses and is a fundamental element of therapies that help people overcome anxiety and phobias.
4. Reflecting on our own mortality can inspire profound changes in our priorities, worldviews, and actions, leading to more meaningful lives.

Self-Reflection Exercises:

1. Identify a fear you have that may be learned and consider how it has affected your decision-making or behavior. Where does this fear originate?
2. Imagine a scenario where you face your identified fear and visualize overcoming it successfully. Note the feelings and thoughts that arise during this mental practice.

Activity:

1. Create a visualization practice schedule for a week, dedicating a few minutes each day to mentally rehearse a task or confront a fear.

15

Self-Discipline

Self-Discipline is an essential aspect of personal growth that both challenges and enriches our journey toward becoming better versions of ourselves. Being disciplined isn't just about denying ourselves the pleasures of the moment; it's crucial for achieving our long-term dreams and improving the overall quality of our lives.

Self-discipline is a powerful tool that frees us from the grip of our impulses and fears. Many barriers we face in life exist only in our minds. By pushing past these mental boundaries, we gain a deeper understanding of ourselves and foster personal growth. This process involves breaking down our old selves and rebuilding into who we aspire to be, despite the inherent risks and discomfort involved. When we step out of our comfort zones and face our fears, we unlock potential that's been lying dormant within us.

A central point of this chapter deals with regulating behavior and making decisions that benefit our future selves. We explore the concept of delayed punishment and how our brains are wired to prioritize immediate rewards over future benefits. This evolutionary trait, while once beneficial, now contributes to modern issues of impulsivity and lack of self-control. Understanding this helps us realize why we struggle with self-discipline and how we can work to improve it.

The chapter concludes with insights into strengthening self-control through deliberate practice and training. Neuroscience shows that self-control can be enhanced much like a muscle, through consistent effort and adequate rest. The chapter wraps up by offering practical tips on how to train our "self-discipline muscle." Applying these strategies can lead to significant changes in how we handle our daily tasks and chase our biggest goals. This fresh understanding of self-discipline paves the way for not only achieving personal growth but also living a more deliberate and satisfying life.

Key Takeaways:

1. Growth begins at the end of your comfort zone. Embracing challenges and facing our fears isn't just about taking risks—it's a fundamental part of becoming the best version of ourselves.
2. Self-discipline is key to achieving lasting success and deep personal satisfaction.
3. The pursuit of immediate gratification often leads to harmful habits. Learning to resist these impulses is crucial for self-improvement.

4. Each decision we make today shapes our tomorrow. By making choices with our future in mind, we pave the way for a life filled with achievements and free of regrets.
5. Self-control is like a muscle—it grows stronger with use, but it also needs time to recover.

Self-Reflection Exercises:

1. Reflect on a time you stepped out of your comfort zone. How did it affect your personal growth?
2. Consider a habit you have that is oriented towards instant gratification. How could this be impacting your long-term goals?

Activities:

1. Create a "future self" journal entry. Detail where you want to be and how present actions can lead to that future.
2. Pick a reward for yourself that you can only receive after completing a certain task or reaching a goal.
3. Begin a habit of waiting at least five minutes before engaging in your favorite activity (i.e., eating your favorite meal, etc.) in order to strengthen your self-control muscle.

16

Problem-Solving

In Chapter Sixteen, "Problem-Solving: The Blueprints of Ambition," we explore the inevitability of life's challenges and how our approach to problem-solving shapes our personal growth. From the moment we are born, we are presented with obstacles that test our resolve and capacity for change. These challenges, far from being purely negative, serve as crucial opportunities for self-improvement. Motivational speakers, gurus, and spiritual leaders often emphasize that self-betterment involves correcting our errors and steering ourselves toward becoming the best versions of ourselves. This process requires a persistent and determined attitude towards finding solutions.

Our journey begins with the simple yet profound example of learning to walk. As infants, we encounter failure repeatedly but persevere until we succeed. This early lesson teaches us that failure is merely a temporary state and that growth necessitates stepping out of our comfort zones, embracing pain, and pushing through failure to achieve success. These experiences provide us with the first blueprints for ambition, demonstrating that unwavering persistence is key to overcoming obstacles.

As we grow older, the problems we face become more complex. We often wish for a life devoid of problems, failing to recognize that certain challenges are essential for growth. While extreme human suffering could be eliminated to improve civilization, the everyday adversities we encounter can be transformed into opportunities for learning and empowerment. By understanding and changing our thoughts and behaviors, we can alleviate much of our suffering. Research supports that positive emotions can improve mood states and mitigate stress effects.

However, as adults, we often lose the persistent attitude we had as children. Faced with discomfort, many of us avoid addressing our problems, preferring temporary relief over long-term resolution. This avoidance leads to chronic stress, depression, and immobility, trapping us in our comfort zones and leaving us unprepared for inevitable challenges.

Reflecting on my own experiences, I've realized that many of our problems are familiar equations we already know how to solve. The skills we develop in school, for instance, go beyond factual knowledge; they teach us valuable problem-solving strategies. Completing a degree involves managing time, organizing life, and enlisting resources—skills that apply to various life situations. The confidence gained from solving difficult problems is an invaluable tool that extends beyond academic achievements.

To overcome present conflicts, we can recall past successes

and the strategies we employed. Our innate problem-solving abilities, learned from infancy, remain with us throughout life. By reigniting our dormant potential and believing in ourselves, we can tackle any challenge with the same persistence that helped us take our first steps. Embracing this childlike confidence and persistence empowers us to face life's difficulties head-on, allowing us to navigate our paths with freedom and resilience.

Key Takeaways:

1. Challenges are not just unavoidable; they are essential. They push us to grow and improve, adding depth and strength to our character.
2. Think about when you learned to walk. Those early steps set the stage for a lifelong habit of persistence and creative problem-solving.
3. If we handle adversity well, we can turn it into a strength. This not only promotes happiness but also enhances our overall well-being.
4. The problem-solving skills we gain from our education and experiences are incredibly useful. They can be applied to nearly any situation in life.

Self-Reflection Exercises:

1. Consider a problem you've been avoiding and explore the reasons behind your avoidance. What temporary comfort does this avoidance provide, and what are the long-term consequences?
2. Identify a past educational or life experience that enhanced

your problem-solving skills. How can those skills be applied to a current situation you face?

Activities:

1. Create a "Problem-Solving Blueprint" that maps out steps taken when confronting a new challenge, incorporating lessons from past successes and failures.
2. Develop a "Skill Transfer" project, identifying a skill learned in an unrelated context (such as an academic setting) and brainstorm ways to apply it to a real-world problem.

17

Persistence

As Teddy Roosevelt famously said, it's better to try and fail than to have never tried at all. This idea is central to the chapter, emphasizing that true defeat lies in never attempting to achieve our higher goals and desires. The mind, often our greatest adversary, conjures fears and doubts that prevent us from even starting our journey towards our aspirations. We imagine endless ways to fail rather than succeed, leading to self-defeat that halts our progress before it begins.

Our doubts and dreams share the same birthplace—the mind. The power to create both means we can choose which to follow. Self-defeat manifests as our mind attempting to protect us from pain by highlighting our perceived inadequacies. However, avoiding risk entirely means missing out on potential growth and achievement. Preparation and foresight are crucial, but we must also accept that some level of risk is inherent in any worthwhile pursuit.

Challenges should be viewed as opportunities for growth rather than reasons to quit. The hedonic notion of maximizing pleasure and minimizing pain neglects the importance of adversity in achieving success. Adversity, symbolized by the proverbial "bumps in the road," is essential for learning and growth. It's through hardship that we either throw in the towel or become stronger.

Highlight reels on social media often propagate the myth that success comes easily to those with inherent talents. This distorted view discourages others by obscuring the struggles behind the success. True success is born from persistence and the ability to adapt and find meaning in our struggles. The only "bad" experience is one that offers no lessons or opportunities for growth.

The chapter explores stories of individuals who transformed their pain into extraordinary achievements. Tommy Caldwell, a rock climber, overcame the trauma of a kidnapping and a severe injury to conquer the seemingly impossible climb of the Dawn Wall. Similarly, David Goggins, an ultramarathon runner and former Navy SEAL, turned his traumatic childhood experiences into an unstoppable drive for self-improvement.

These examples from athletics, chosen for their well-documented research base, illustrate that the mindset required for physical achievements can be applied to other areas of life. Pain and adversity, often seen as negative, are integral to growth and success. Persistence ensures that failure is temporary, teaching us that opposites like pleasure and pain are inseparable.

The chapter concludes by emphasizing that while extraordinary challenges like those faced by Caldwell and Goggins are not required for personal growth, their stories provide blueprints for overcoming obstacles. Persistence is about knowing when to pause, reevaluate, and continue. By developing a sense of agency and autonomy, we can prevent failure from becoming defeat and use our struggles to propel us towards our goals.

Key Takeaways:

1. True defeat comes from not attempting to achieve goals, not from the act of failing itself.
2. Your own mind can be your biggest obstacle. It's essential to conquer the self-doubt that stops you from succeeding.
3. Think of failure as a growth opportunity. Instead of seeing failure as a setback, view it as an important step towards your development.
4. Social media often portrays an incomplete picture of success. It tends to show only the highlights, skipping over the struggles and perseverance that are often behind true success.
5. Inspirational journeys like those of Tommy Caldwell and David Goggins reveal the incredible power of persistence. Their experiences demonstrate how enduring through tough times can lead to extraordinary achievements.

Self-Reflection Exercises:

1. Consider your definition of failure and success. How can redefining these terms in your own life encourage growth and resilience?

2. Identify an area in your life where you have experienced self-defeat. What steps can you take to overcome this mindset and pursue your goals despite the potential for failure?

Activities:

1. Write a letter to yourself from the perspective of a future you who has overcome current fears and succeeded. What advice would this future self-give you?
2. Create a "failure resume" listing past failures and what you learned from each, highlighting how they contributed to your personal growth.

18

Methods of Change

This chapter explores various techniques designed to transform ourselves and our circumstances, highlighting the fluid boundaries between methods of acceptance and methods of change. These categorizations serve as guidelines to balance order and chaos in our lives, aiming for inner freedom and choice.

The chapter emphasizes the importance of sleep hygiene. Quality sleep is vital for energy, alertness, and clarity. Research underscores its role in immune function, mental health, and overall well-being, with sleep deprivation linked to increased risks of obesity, diabetes, heart disease, and mental health disorders. The necessity of getting eight to ten hours of sleep per night is stressed to maintain optimal performance and health.

Diet and nutrition are explored next, with a focus on the profound impact of food on mental and physical health. While no universal diet fits all, whole, natural foods are emphasized. The chapter highlights the benefits of probiotics and a balanced gut-brain axis for mental health and points to Mediterranean and Japanese diets as models for healthy eating.

Exercise is another critical component. Physical activity enhances mood, cognitive function, and neuroplasticity. Regular exercise has antidepressant effects comparable to psychotherapy and significantly reduces the risk of early death and morbidity. The text encourages integrating enjoyable activities into exercise routines for consistency and enjoyment.

The importance of socialization is addressed, noting that our mental, physical, and spiritual health depends significantly on our social bonds. The chapter discusses the decline in social connectedness in Western culture and its impact on mental health, advocating for the rekindling of genuine connections. Positive social support is crucial for healing and well-being, extending beyond therapeutic relationships to include family, friends, and community involvement.

Time management is another essential topic. Effective time management involves setting goals, making to-do lists, scheduling, prioritizing tasks, and learning to delegate. A sense of control over time management leads to reduced stress and improved mental health. Practical strategies like maintaining a general to-do list, daily focused planning, and weekly goal setting are introduced to manage responsibilities effectively.

Finally, the chapter discusses strengthening willpower. Practical tips include delaying gratification, making mundane tasks enjoyable, and drawing inspiration from role models to build self-control. These methods, along with meditation and exercise, are presented as powerful tools for personal transformation. By integrating these practices into our lives, we can overcome challenges, improve our understanding, and ultimately achieve a balanced, fulfilling existence.

Key Takeaways:

1. Prioritizing sufficient sleep is crucial, as it strengthens the immune system, enhances mental functions, and reduces the risk of chronic diseases.
2. Eating a diet rich in whole foods while minimizing processed items significantly improves both mental and physical health.
3. Regular exercise can uplift your mood and enhance brain function, proving as effective as psychotherapy and antidepressants.
4. Maintaining social connections is essential for mental, physical, and spiritual well-being, helping to prevent the rise of mental health issues.
5. Effective time management boosts personal autonomy and reduces stress, enhancing overall mental health and quality of life.

Self-Reflection Exercises:

1. Reflect on your current sleep habits: Are you getting enough sleep? How might you improve your sleep hygiene?
2. Think about your dietary choices. What specific whole or minimally processed foods could you incorporate into your

diet?
3. Reflect on your exercise routine. Are you making time to get your heart pumping? What enjoyable activities could you incorporate to maintain consistency?
4. What kinds of social interactions do you find most fulfilling, and how can you create more opportunities for those?
5. What are your current strategies for managing time, and how could you improve them to feel more in control of your life?

Activities:

1. Create a sleep diary, noting your bedtime, wake-up time, and quality of sleep. Identify patterns and plan adjustments to improve sleep hygiene.
2. Plan a week's menu incorporating elements of the Mediterranean or Japanese diet, focusing on whole foods and reducing processed food intake.
3. Schedule and commit to a 30-minute exercise session three times a week, choosing activities you enjoy, and track your mood before and after each session.
4. Plan a social event or activity where you can connect with others, such as a community meet-up, sports game, or volunteer work.
5. Develop a time management plan that includes setting weekly goals, creating daily to-do lists, and using a planner to organize and track your activities and goals.

IV

Part Four: Understanding

19

Generating Self-Awareness

The interplay between self-knowledge and personal growth is profound, and our understanding—or lack thereof—of our inner world can significantly shape our life's course. While machines have gauges and measuring instruments to signal their needs, we humans often lack such clear indicators, leaving us unaware of our true condition until problems escalate.

Society often fails to encourage self-awareness, leaving us susceptible to what is known in Hinduism and Buddhism as "avidyā," a Sanskrit term for misconceptions that cloud our self-perception and limit our potential. These are the stories we tell ourselves, the narratives that can lead us astray. I, like many others, have personally struggled with these misconceptions and have seen firsthand how they can hold us back.

Interoception, our ability to perceive physical sensations, is a powerful tool in this journey of self-discovery. These signals, the closest we have to a machine's gauges, form the foundation of core self-awareness: the immediate sense of how we feel physically and emotionally. However, self-awareness isn't confined to just the present moment. It encompasses our understanding of ourselves over time—our history, aspirations, and evolving narrative. Both forms of awareness are essential, yet stress and trauma can disrupt them, distorting our internal compass.

By actively cultivating interoception, we harness our personal agency and gain greater control over our lives. By mapping our internal world, we can navigate life's stresses, differentiating between distress, which debilitates, and eustress, which motivates. Equipped with these concepts, we can face challenges with newfound clarity, redefining our limits and expanding our horizons. Through deeper self-awareness, we don't just survive; we thrive, unlocking a fuller understanding of ourselves and our potential. This chapter invites us on this vital journey of self-discovery, serving as a reminder that the path to external achievements often begins with internal exploration and self-understanding.

Key Takeaways:

1. Knowing yourself is key to personal growth. By recognizing what we're good at and where we need improvement, we can strike a healthy balance between accepting ourselves and striving to change.
2. Unlike a car's dashboard that shows its status, we don't have clear indicators for our mental and emotional states. This means we need to actively engage in understanding what's happening inside us.
3. Interoception is your secret tool for better self-awareness.

It helps you recognize and understand the signals your body sends about your feelings and emotions.
4. It's important to know the difference between two types of stress: distress, which wears you down, and eustress, which can actually motivate and energize you. Understanding this can help you manage stress in a way that supports your growth.
5. Practices like meditation and mindful reflection are like mapping your internal landscape. These tools can lead to a deeper understanding of yourself, giving you more control over your life and a greater sense of freedom.

Self-Reflection Exercises:

1. Reflect on an occasion when you surpassed what you believed was your limit. What can you learn from this experience about your potential?
2. Consider the distinctions between distress and eustress. Identify a recent stressor in your life and categorize it as one or the other. Reflect on how this categorization changes your perception of the stressor.

Activities:

1. Practice interoception by focusing on your bodily sensations during a routine activity like eating or exercising and note any new insights.
2. Engage in a "mapping" exercise: create a physical representation (like a map) of your mental state, including emotions, stressors, and comfort zones.
3. Conduct a stress audit of your past week to identify sources

of distress and eustress, and develop a plan for transforming the former into the latter or mitigating its effects.

20

Methods of Self-Understanding

In Chapter Twenty, "Methods of Self-Understanding," we explore self-regulation, or emotion regulation, which involves balancing internal conflicts between order and chaos. This ability to stabilize our moods and manage emotions is essential for functioning well psychologically, physiologically, and interpersonally. This chapter serves as a guide to practices that help us transcend limitations and understand our inner selves.

Psychotherapy is a key method of self-understanding, emphasizing mental causation, emotion control, and free will. Successful psychotherapy enhances one's capacity for self-determined decisions. Neuroscience shows that intentional emotion regulation activates specific brain regions, demonstrating that our conscious minds shape our behaviors. Psychotherapy, grounded in the idea that changing our thoughts can change our feelings, fosters emotional control in a safe, supportive environment. Research shows that psychotherapy is as effective as medication for many psychiatric conditions and often more effective when combined with medication. Psychodynamic psychotherapy helps clients articulate their inner feelings, aiming to increase self-awareness and control. Cognitive Behavioral Therapy (CBT), developed by Albert Ellis and Aaron Beck, targets cognitive distortions and alleviates distress through adaptive techniques.

Finding the right therapist is crucial. Competent therapists exhibit genuineness, honesty, empathy, cultural competence, self-awareness, humor, warmth, and maintain healthy boundaries. Methods for finding a therapist include using insurance directories, online reviews, recommendations, and trusting your intuition during consultations.

Expressive writing, such as journaling, enhances self-understanding by improving emotional well-being and clarifying life values and goals. James Pennebaker's research supports the benefits of expressive writing for psychological and physical health. Writing about concerns and emotions facilitates deeper self-awareness and personal growth.

Inventory, a practice from Alcoholics Anonymous, encourages honest appraisals of one's actions and circumstances, improving social health by promoting responsibility and empathy. It helps individuals acknowledge their role in conflicts and prevent future issues.

Biofeedback uses electronic devices to reflect physiological functions, helping individuals learn to control them consciously.

Research shows biofeedback improves heart rate variability (HRV), linked to better self-regulation, impulse control, and decision-making. Even without electronic devices, paying close attention to bodily sensations during emotional experiences can enhance self-understanding and control.

In conclusion, these methods—psychotherapy, expressive writing, inventory, and biofeedback—offer valuable tools to overcome challenges and improve well-being. By increasing self-awareness and emotional regulation, we can better navigate our internal worlds, leading to more balanced and fulfilling lives.

Key Takeaways:

1. Self-regulation is crucial for well-being. It promotes emotional balance, reduces stress, and improves overall mental and physical health.
2. Psychotherapy unlocks self-awareness: Engaging in psychotherapy can be transformative, enhancing our understanding of our own thoughts and feelings and giving us the tools to manage them. This not only improves emotional control but also bolsters our sense of independence.
3. Whether it's uncovering deep-seated emotional patterns with psychodynamic therapy or restructuring negative thoughts and behaviors through cognitive behavioral therapy (CBT), different therapeutic approaches can address a variety of psychological challenges effectively.
4. Regularly practicing expressive writing and keeping a personal inventory are powerful self-help tools. They help us delve deeper into our psyche, understand our emotional triggers, and track our personal growth over time.

5. Biofeedback is a technique that uses real-time displays of bodily functions, like heart rate and muscle tension, to teach us how to take control of our physical responses. This can have a profound effect on our mental and physical health, helping us manage stress and anxiety more effectively.

Self-Reflection Exercises:

1. Reflect on a challenging emotional experience and identify the strategies you used to manage it. Were they effective? What other strategies could you have tried
2. Consider your current beliefs and behaviors. Which of these align with your values and long-term goals? Which might need adjusting, and why?
3. Write about an interpersonal conflict and critically analyze your role in it. How could you have approached it differently? What strategies could you use in future situations to promote healthier communication and resolution?

Activities:

1. Create a checklist based on the inventory method to evaluate daily interactions and personal behavior. This checklist could include questions like: "Did I react impulsively today?" or "Was I able to communicate my needs effectively?"
2. If possible, obtain a biofeedback device (e.g., heart rate variability monitor) and practice using it to become more aware of your physiological responses to stress and emotions. Many affordable options are available for home use.

21

The Middle Path Between Acceptance and Change

The final chapter of this book invites you to join me in a profound exploration that began at the New York Hall of Science, where a friend and I marveled at the Galton Board. This captivating observation paralleled the Buddhist principle of the middle path, beautifully encapsulating the delicate balance between order and chaos. Delving deeper into this concept, we explore the powerful essence of the serenity prayer by Reinhold Niebuhr, which urges us to accept what cannot be changed, courageously change what can, and cultivate the wisdom to distinguish between the two.

This framework challenges us to question our perspectives on life's unchangeable elements and those within our power to alter. By examining the pitfalls of absolute acceptance and the dangers of an incessant drive for change, we uncover a balanced approach to living.

Throughout this discussion, we engage with various methods

and examples that illustrate our themes. For instance, the analogy of open-world video games serves as a modern metaphor for life's expansive possibilities. These games offer boundless freedom yet often lack direction, mirroring the paradoxes we face in our lives. Here, we learn that a life filled with purpose and challenges, much like a well-designed game, leads to fulfillment and growth.

As we conclude this journey, we reflect on the elusive nature of life's ultimate purpose. The insights gained from understanding the interplay between acceptance and change do not offer definitive answers but guide us toward greater personal freedom and self-determination. By embracing this balanced approach, we not only navigate life's complexities with greater ease but also engage more deeply with the world around us, enhancing our understanding and enriching our experiences.

This chapter, therefore, is not merely a summary of concepts; it is an invitation to embody the wisdom of the middle path. As we step forward, we carry forward the courage to change, the serenity to accept, and the wisdom to know the difference—empowering us to live freely and fully in a world of infinite possibilities. May this wisdom guide you on your own unique path toward greater freedom and fulfillment.

Key Takeaways:

1. The Galton Board metaphorically represents the balance of order and chaos, similar to the middle path in Buddhism.
2. Finding balance is vital: extreme acceptance can lead to passivity, while excessive pursuit of change can result in

burnout.
3. The serenity prayer highlights the importance of discerning between what can and cannot be changed.
4. Understanding the interplay between acceptance and change is key to personal growth and freedom.
5. Unconstrained freedom, as seen in open-world video games, can sometimes lead to a lack of direction and meaning, highlighting the importance of purposeful engagement with the world.

Self-Reflection Exercises:

1. Reflect on an area of your life where you lean towards either extreme acceptance or extreme change, and consider how a balance of both might improve your situation. What are some small steps you could take to cultivate more balance in this area
2. Identify a current situation where you need to apply acceptance, change, or a combination of both. What aspects of the situation can you accept, and what can you actively work to change?
3. Write about a time when having too many choices or too much freedom left you feeling overwhelmed, unsatisfied, or directionless. What could you have done differently to navigate this situation more effectively?

Activity:

1. Role-play a scenario with a partner where one person advocates for change and the other for acceptance. Then discuss the middle path that could be taken.

Made in the USA
Middletown, DE
27 July 2024